JOHN W. SCHAUM
THEORY LESSONS
BOOK TWO

D1317012

John W. Schaum Theory Lessons

1. MUSIC THEORY FOR THE EARLIEST BEGINNER

There is a need for music theory in the earliest stages of piano study. *Book One of the John Schaum Theory Lessons* may begin at the very first piano lesson.

2. MIDDLE C APPROACH

These theory lessons use the middle C approach, so they correlate very closely with the actual learning steps of the early stages of piano study.

3. SAVES TIME

The student learns theory with a minimum of the teacher's time. Adequate explanatory remarks precede each new step so that the student can do the assignment without lengthy explanation by the teacxher. The teacher can then devote the majority of lesson time to the student's piano playing.

4. DEVELOPS STUDENT'S INITIATIVE

After reading the explanations given with each lesson, most students need no extra help from the teacher. The assignment can be prepared at home or at the lesson and left with the teacher for correction, thereby developing the student's initiative as well as conserving valuable lesson time.

5. CLASS OR PRIVATE INSTRUCTION

The John W. Schaum Theory Lessons are suitable for class lessons as well as for private instruction.

EL00245A

Lesson 1. Spelling Words with Note Names

Name _____ Date _____ Grade _____

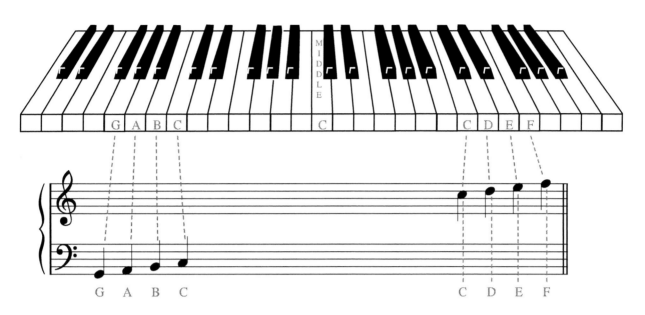

DIRECTIONS: Write the letter names of the following notes.

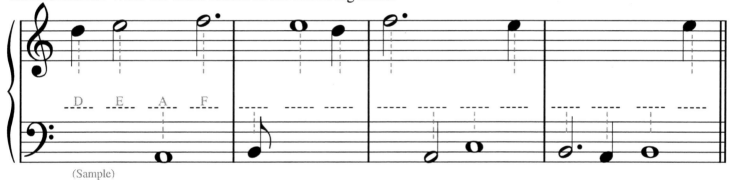

(Sample)

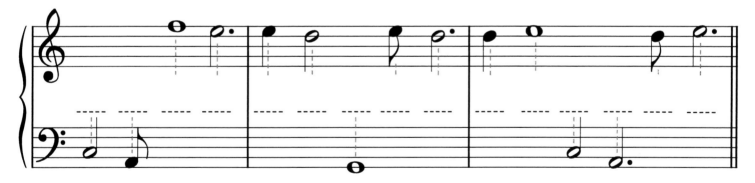

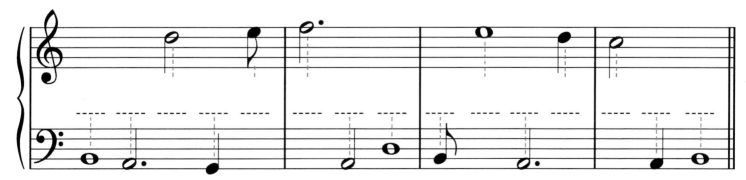

EL00245A

Lesson 2. Note Spelling and Octaves

Name _____ Date _____ Grade _____

DIRECTIONS: Write the notes for each of the following words on both the treble and the bass staff. Make whole notes.

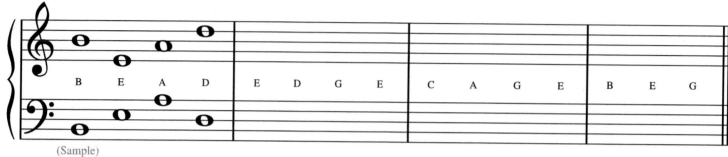

(Sample)

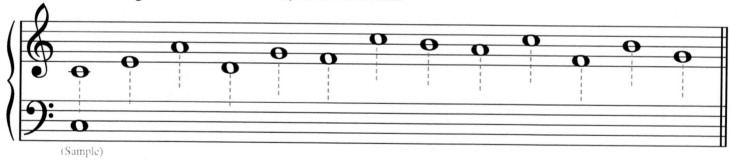

Rewrite the following notes one octave lower, on the bass staff.

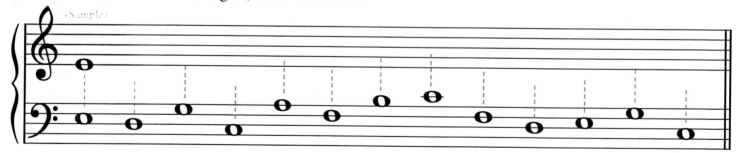

(Sample)

Rewrite these notes one octave higher, on the treble staff.

EL00245A

Lesson 3. Notes and Rests

Name _____ Date _____ Grade _____

Notes

Piano playing is a combination of sound and silence. *Notes* tell us when and where to play the keys. *Rests* tell us when not to play.

Rests

*DIRECTIONS: Below is a series of notes and rests. Write N for note and R for rest.

R   N
----- -----
(Samples)

*Teacher's Note: Do not explain note and rest values in this lesson. The purpose here is simply to distinguish a note from a rest.

EL00245A

Lesson 4. Rest Values

Name _____   Date _____   Grade _____

Rests are signs of silence. They tell us the number of counts that we do *not* play.

A QUARTER Rest ⟋ gets 1 count.

A HALF Rest — gets 2 counts.

A WHOLE Rest — gets 4 counts.

DIRECTIONS: Write the number of counts under each rest.

1   4
---- ----   ----   ----   ----   ----   ----   ----   ----   ----
(Samples)

----   ----   ----   ----   ----   ----   ----   ----   ----   ----

Write the counts below the notes and rests in each measure.

Count: 1   2   3   4
(Sample)

Count:

Count:

Lesson 5. Counting Notes and Rests

Name _____ Date _____ Grade _____

Notes and rests of the same value are counted the same, as shown in this diagram.

Quarter	♩ = 1 count = 𝄽	
Half	𝅗𝅥 = 2 counts = ▬	
Dotted Half	𝅗𝅥. = 3 counts = 𝄽 𝄽 𝄽	
Whole	𝅝 = 4 counts = ▬	

DIRECTIONS: Write the counts below the notes and rests in each measure. Watch for different time signatures.

Note: Most music engravers today avoid the use of half rests in 3/4 time, using two quarter rests instead. However, there is much music in print which includes half rests in 3/4 meter.

Lesson 6. Note Stems

Name _____   Date _____   Grade _____

The stems of notes *below* the middle line go UP - on the *right* side of the note head.

The stems of notes *above* the middle line go DOWN - on the *left* side of the note head.

Study the following examples.

Stems up   Stems down

DIRECTIONS: Change the following whole notes into HALF NOTES (♩) by adding stems. Be sure to put UP stems on the right side of the note and DOWN stems on the left side.

DIRECTIONS: Change the following whole notes into QUARTER NOTES (♩) by filling in each note head and adding a stem. Be careful to draw the stem up or down, on the correct side of the note head.

DIRECTIONS: Change the following whole notes into EIGHTH NOTES. Fill in each note head, add a stem, and add a *flag* (♪). Be careful to put the flags in the correct position, as shown in the samples.

When two or more eighth notes are next to each other, the stems of the eighth notes are often connected with a thick line called a **beam**. Study the samples below.

DIRECTIONS: Change the following whole notes into *pairs* of EIGHTH NOTES. Fill in each note head, add a stem, and connect the stems with beams.

EL00245A

Lesson 7. Rhythm Choices

Name _____ Date _____ Grade _____

DIRECTIONS: In the measures below, change the whole notes into other kinds of notes so that each measure has the correct number of counts. Be careful to draw the stem up or down, on the correct side of the note head. Watch for different time signatures. Write the numbers for the counts on the dotted line below each note.

For example, here are three correct ways to do the sample measure:

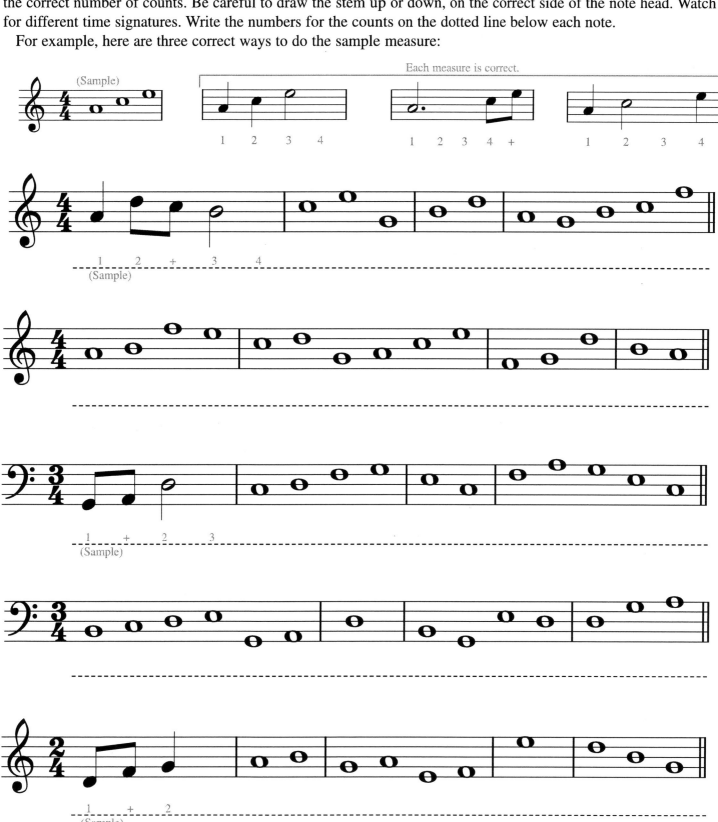

Lesson 8. Counting/Note Location

Name _____ Date _____ Grade _____

DIRECTIONS: Write the numbers for the counts on the dotted line below each note and rest.

1   +   2   3   +   4
(Sample)

DIRECTIONS: Draw a whole note for each letter in both the treble and bass staffs.

(Sample)

| C | A | B | F | A | D | B | E | A | D | B | A | D | G | E |

| D | E | A | F | F | A | C | E | B | E | G | C | A | G | E |

Lesson 9. Counting in Treble and Bass Staffs

Name _____ Date _____ Grade _____

DIRECTIONS: Write the numbers for the counts on the dotted line below each note and rest. Be sure that the counts fit both treble and bass notes. Watch for different time signatures.

1   +   2   +   3
(Sample)

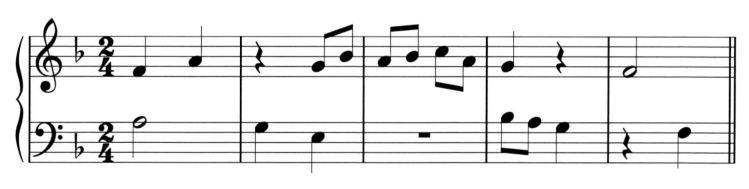

Lesson 10. Note Names Up and Down in the Staffs

Name _____ Date _____ Grade _____

DIRECTIONS: Write the letter name on the dotted line below each note. Watch for the clef signs.

F
(Sample)

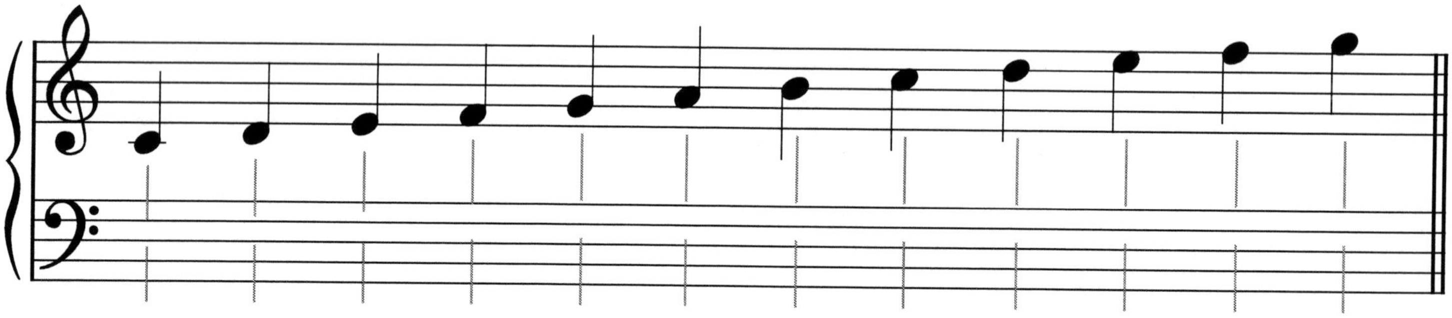

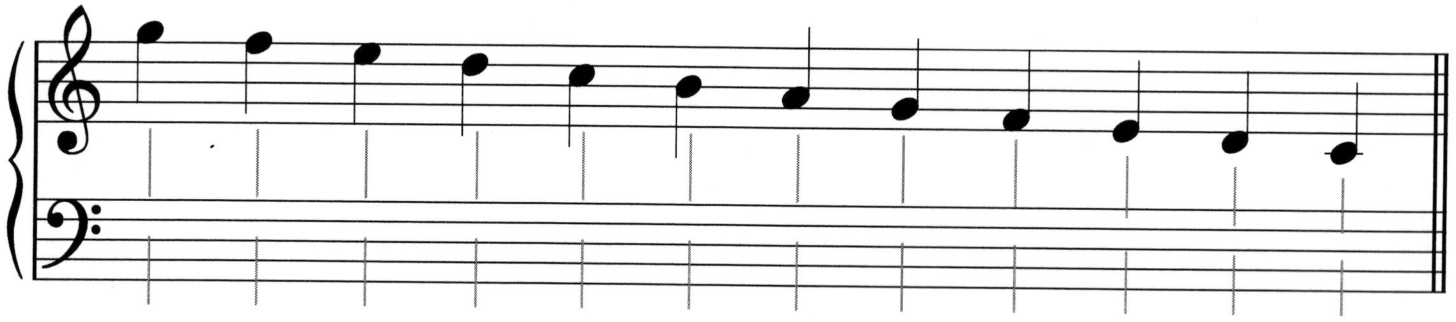

G
(Sample)

EL00245A

Lesson 11. Natural Accents

Name _____   Date _____   Grade _____

A *natural accent* is a pulse that is felt on the first beat of every measure in all time signatures. It is usually an *implied accent that is felt as you play*, but not actually played louder. However, in some styles of music, the natural accent may be played *slightly louder* than other counts in a measure.

DIRECTIONS: In 4/4 time the natural accent occurs on the first count of every measure. Draw a circle around the note on the *first beat* of each measure below.

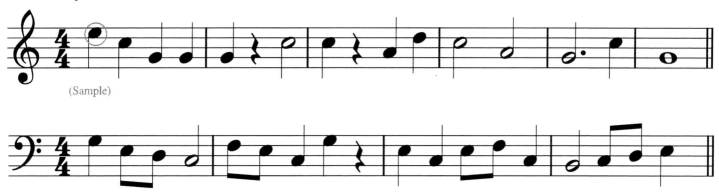

DIRECTIONS: In 2/4 time the natural accent also occurs on the first count of every measure. Draw a circle around the note on the *first beat* of each measure below.

DIRECTIONS: In 3/4 time the natural accent also occurs on the first count of every measure. Draw a circle around the note on the *first beat* of each measure below.

EL00245A

Lesson 12. Tied Notes

Name _____ Date _____ Grade _____

The *tie* is a curved line joining two notes on the same line or space. The second note is not played, but is held for its full value.

DIRECTIONS: In the following measures, wherever a tie occurs, draw an X through the note that you would *not* pla

(Sample)

EL00245A

Lesson 13. The "Inner Aces" (Inner Leger Lines)

Name _____   Date _____   Grade _____

You can easily remember the letter names of the leger lines above the bass staff and below the treble staff by the word ACE.

These leger lines are called the *"inner* aces" because they are *in between* the treble and bass staffs.

DIRECTIONS: Write the letter name on the dotted line below each note. Keep in mind the "inner aces." Notice the leger lines are *in between* the staffs.

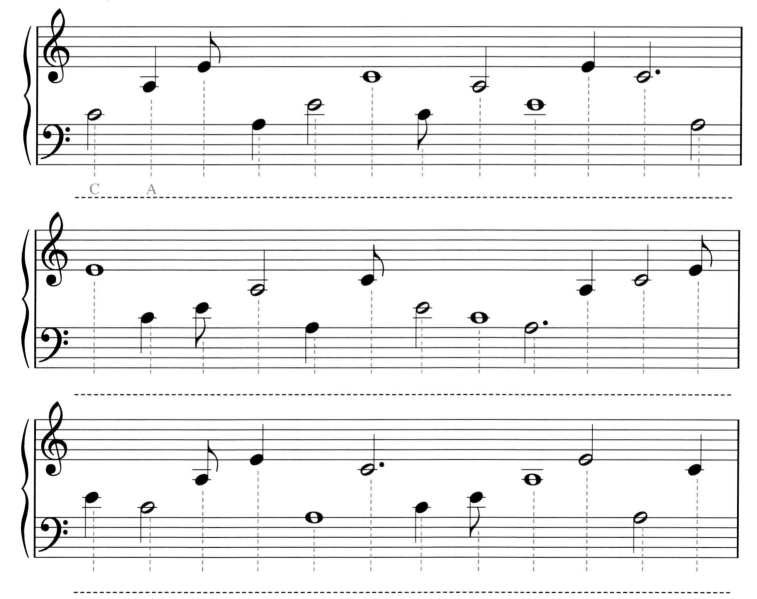

Lesson 14. Spaces Between the Two "Inner Aces"

Name _____ Date _____ Grade _____

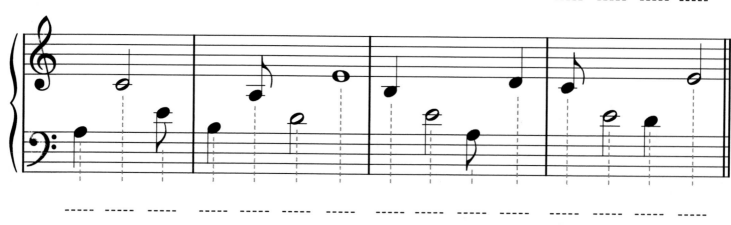

DIRECTIONS: Each measure below spells a word using the notes of the inner leger lines and spaces.
Write the letter name below each note. Think of the two ACES and if a note is in a space, then count up or down from one of the A-C-E lines.

Lesson 15. Ten Musical Riddles

Name _____ Date _____ Grade _____

DIRECTIONS: Write the letter names and you will discover the answers to the riddles.

1. What food comes from cattle?

(Write letter names.) ____ ____ ____ ____

2. What gets a head in the garden?

____ ____ ____ ____ ____ ____ ____

3. What city was home to a storybook thief?

____ ____ ____ ____ ____ ____

4. Scouts do a good one daily.

____ ____ ____ ____

5. What is the nickname of a great American president?

____ ____ ____

6. What do you hate to wash?

____ ____ ____ ____

7. What does the sun do in the evening?

____ ____ ____ ____

8. What do travelers carry?

____ ____ ____ ____ ____ ____ ____

9. What does a comedian tell?

____ ____ ____

10. Where don't you like to go early?

____ ____ ____

Lesson 16. Inner Leger Lines

Name _____ Date _____ Grade _____

Notes for the five keys shown on the keyboard may be written two ways.

1. Below the treble staff (for the right hand).

2. Above the bass staff (for the left hand).

Although the notes are written on different staffs, they will be the same key on the keyboard.

DIRECTIONS: For each of the following treble staff notes, write the same note in the bass staff. Be sure that it is the same key on the keyboard. Make whole notes.

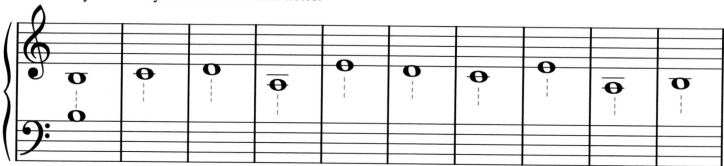

For each of the following bass staff notes, write the same note in the treble staff. Make whole notes.

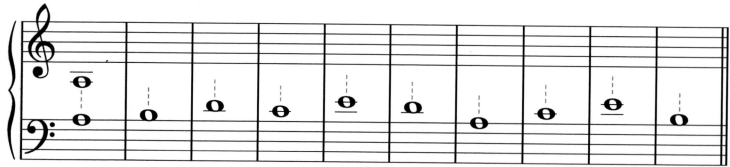

Write the letter names for the following notes.

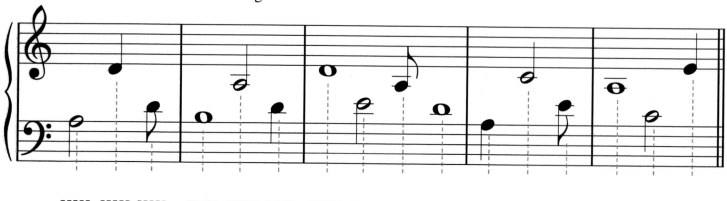

----- ----- -----   ----- ----- -----   ----- ----- ----- -----   ----- ----- -----   ----- ----- -----

EL00245A

Lesson 17. The "Outer Aces" (Outer Leger Lines)

The word ACE also helps you to remember the letter names of the leger lines *below* the bass staff and *above* the treble staff.

These leger lines are called the "*outer* aces" because they are *outside* of the treble and bass staffs.

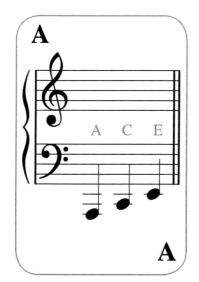

DIRECTIONS: Write the letter name on the dotted line below each note. Keep in mind the "outer aces." Notice that the leger lines are *outside* of the staffs.

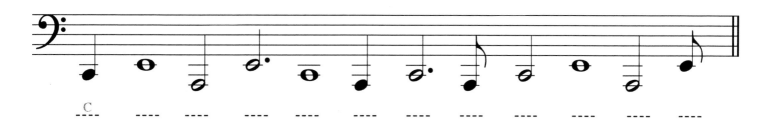

DIRECTIONS: Write the letter names on the dotted lines below. Remember the "outer aces."

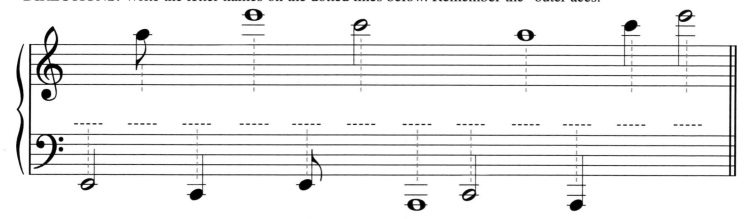

EL00245A

Lesson 18. Spaces Between the Two "Outer Aces"

Name _____ Date _____ Grade _____

DIRECTIONS: Each measure below spells a word using the notes of the outer leger lines and spaces. Write the letter name for each note. Think of the two ACES, and if a note is in a space, then count up or down from one of the A-C-E lines.

Lesson 19. The "Four Aces" (Inner and Outer Leger Lines)

Name _____ Date _____ Grade _____

The "four aces" will help you to remember the *inner* leger lines and *outer* leger lines.
See Lessons 13 and 17 for more information.

INNER ACES
(*In between* the treble and bass staffs)

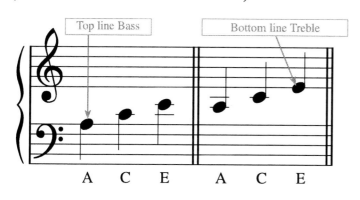

OUTER ACES
(*Outside* the treble and bass staffs)

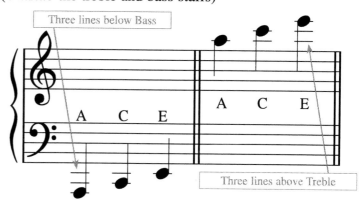

EASY ACES - THINGS TO REMEMBER

1. INNER ACES
   a. The *bass* ACE *begins* on the *top line* of the bass staff.
   b. The *treble* ACE *ends* on the *bottom line* of the treble staff.

2. OUTER ACES
   a. The *bass* ACE is on the three leger lines *below* the bass staff.
   b. The *treble* ACE is on the three leger lines *above* the treble staff.

3. All four ACES read upward.

4. All four ACES are always *lines*, not spaces.

Lesson 20. "Four Aces" Musical Spelling Quiz

Name _____ Date _____ Grade _____

DIRECTIONS: The notes below are a mixture of inner and outer leger lines and spaces. Write the letter name on the dotted line below each note. Each measure spells a different word. Keep the "four aces" in mind.

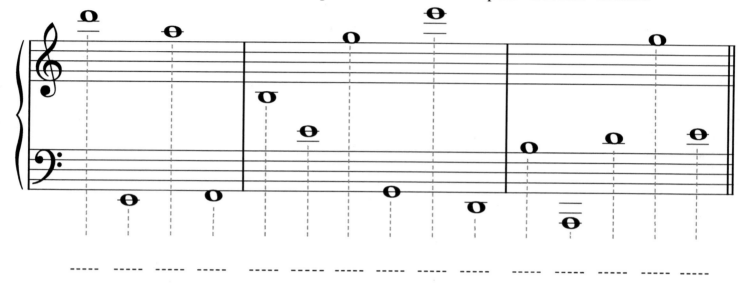

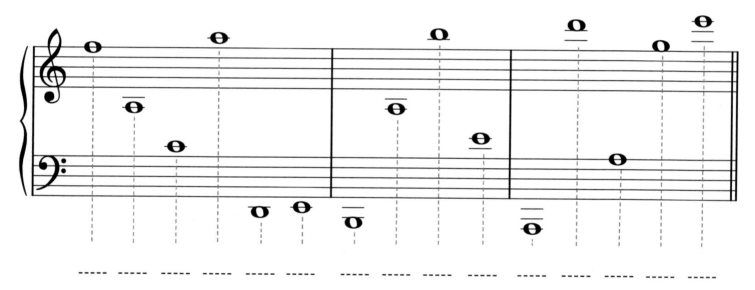

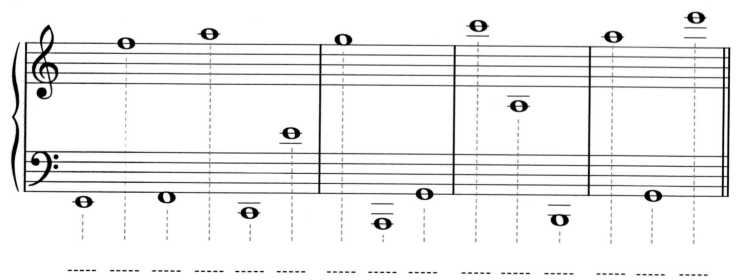

Lesson 21. Key Finding Game

Name _____ Date _____ Grade _____

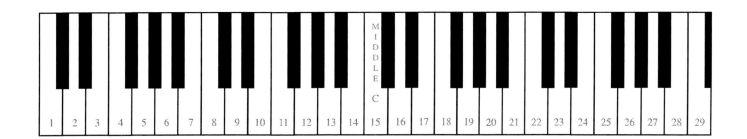

DIRECTIONS: Find the following notes on the keyboard above. Then write the correct *number* beneath each note. Watch for clef changes.

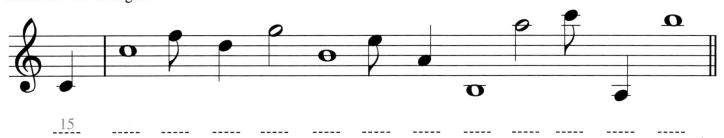

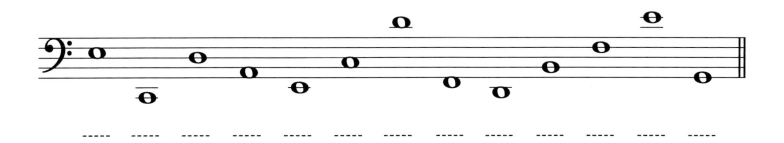

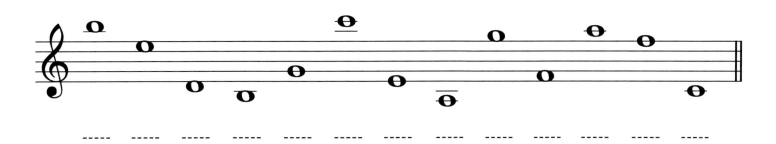

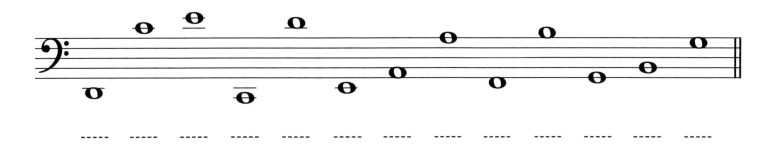

EL00245A

Lesson 22. Octaves (Up and Down)

Name _____ Date _____ Grade _____

DIRECTIONS: Draw each of the following notes in four different places. Use whole notes.

DIRECTIONS: Draw a note *one octave above* each of the following notes. Use whole notes.

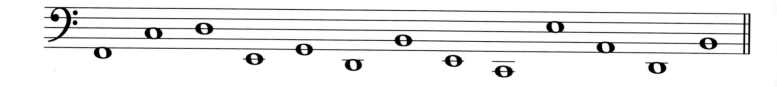

DIRECTIONS: Draw a note *one octave below* each of the following notes. Use whole notes.

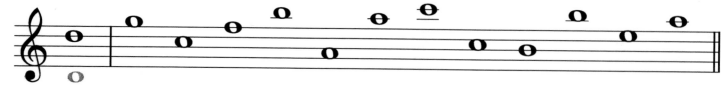

Lesson 23. Half Steps and Whole Steps

Name _____ Date _____ Grade _____

A HALF STEP is the distance from key to key (with NO key in between).

A WHOLE STEP is the distance from key to key (with ONE key in between).

DIRECTIONS: Below is a series of half steps and whole steps involving black and white keys.
Write (H) for each half step; write (W) for each whole step.

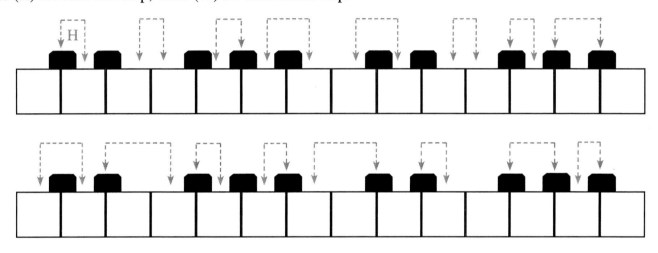

A **sharp** (♯) moves a note UP *one half step*.

A **flat** (♭) moves a note DOWN *one half step*.

DIRECTIONS: Below is a series of sharps and flats. Write U (up) under each sharp; write D (down) under each flat.

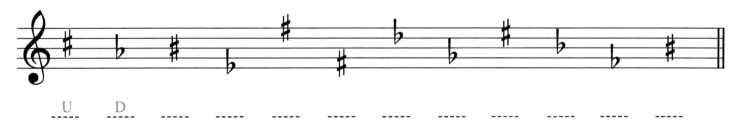

EL00245A

Lesson 24. Sharps, Flats and Half Steps

Name _____ Date _____ Grade _____

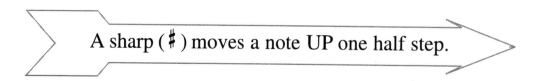

A sharp (♯) moves a note UP one half step.

DIRECTIONS: In the squares below, write the letter name for each of the following notes with sharps. Notice that some sharps are *on white keys*.

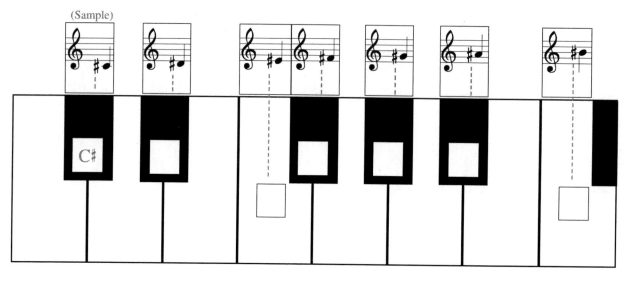

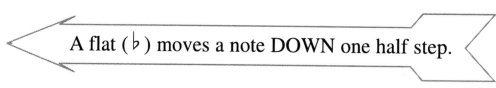

A flat (♭) moves a note DOWN one half step.

DIRECTIONS: In the squares below, write the letter name for each of the following notes with flats. Notice that some flats are *on white keys*.

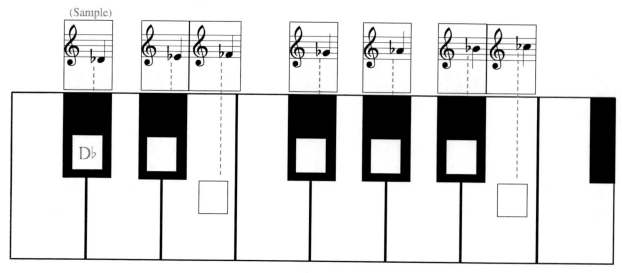

EL00245A

Lesson 25. Sharp and Flat Puzzle

Name _____ Date _____ Grade _____

DIRECTIONS: Find the following notes on the keyboard above. Then write the correct *number* beneath each note.
Remember, a *white key* can also be a sharp or a flat.

EL00245A

Lesson 26. Mixed Sharps, Flats and Naturals

Name _____ Date _____ Grade _____

Good Advice: Be ♯, not ♭, and act ♮!

DIRECTIONS: Find the following notes on the keyboard above. Then write the correct *number* beneath each note. Remember, a *white key* can also be a sharp or a flat.

Lesson 27. Discovering Mistakes

Name _____ Date _____ Grade _____

DIRECTIONS: In the measures below, some of the notes are wrong. Draw an X through the wrong notes. The sample is marked correctly.

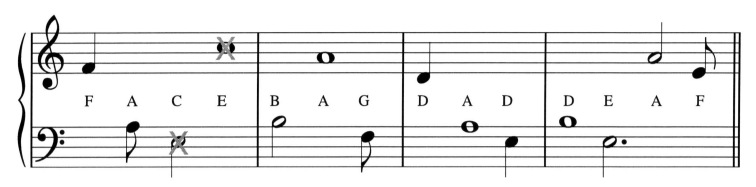

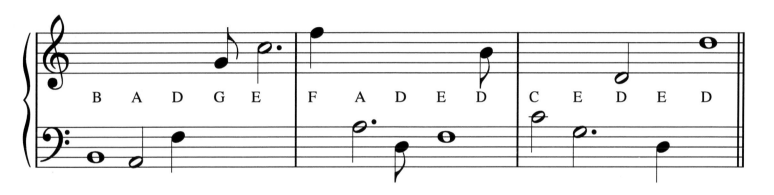

Lesson 28. Finding Counts and Bar Lines

Name _____ Date _____ Grade _____

DIRECTIONS: Draw a circle around the note or rest which is *at the beginning* of the THIRD count in each measure. Study the sample.

DIRECTIONS: The measure bar lines are missing in the following staffs. Draw in bar lines so that each measure will have the correct number of counts. Watch for different time signatures.

EL00245A

Lesson 29. Line and Space Skips

Name _____ Date _____ Grade _____

DIRECTIONS: Notes on lines always *skip a letter* and *skip a white key*. Write the letter name for each note *in two places*: 1) on the dotted line below the staff. 2) on the keyboard diagram. Study the sample.

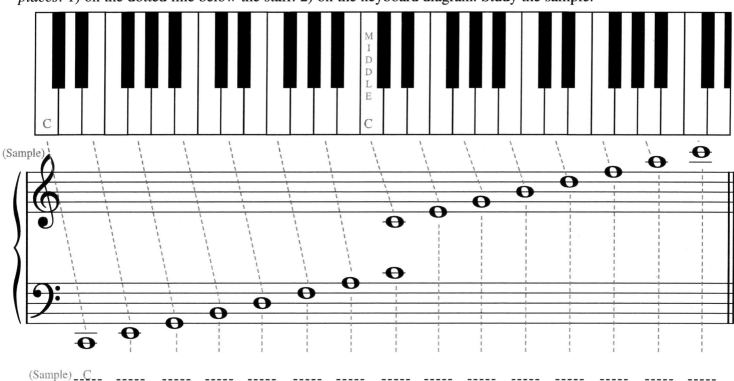

(Sample) C _____ _____ _____ _____ _____ _____ _____ _____ _____ _____ _____ _____ _____ _____

DIRECTIONS: Notes in spaces also always *skip a letter* and *skip a white key*. Write the letter name for each note *in two places*: 1) on the dotted line below the staff. 2) on the keyboard diagram. Study the sample.

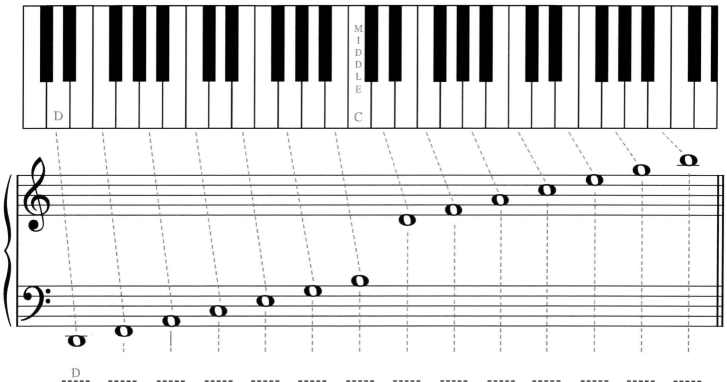

D _____ _____ _____ _____ _____ _____ _____ _____ _____ _____ _____ _____ _____

EL00245A

Lesson 30. Theory Quiz

Name _____   Date _____   Grade _____

DIRECTIONS: Complete each sentence by drawing a circle around the correct answer.

SAMPLE: ♩ This is called a .... rest   (note)   clef   sharp   flat

1. ♩ This note is a .... half   whole   eighth   quarter   sixteenth

2. ♯ This is a .... rest   staff   natural   sharp   flat

3. ≣ These five lines are called a .... measure   staff   clef   brace   natural

4. o This note is a .... whole   half   eighth   quarter   sixteenth

5. 𝄞 This is a .... bass clef   treble clef   brace   measure   natural

6. ▬ This rest is a .... sixteenth   half   whole   eighth   quarter

7. ♭ This is a .... flat   sharp   natural   quarter   sixteenth

8. ♫ These notes are .... halves   wholes   sixteenths   eighths   quarters

9. 𝄽 This rest is a .... half   quarter   eighth   whole   sixteenth

10. ♮ This is a .... sharp   flat   staff   natural   clef

11. ≣ This vertical line is a .... sharp   bar line   natural   note

12. 𝅗𝅥 This note is a .... whole   quarter   half   sixteenth   eighth

13. ▭ This is a .... fence   measure   flat   note   key

14. ▬ This rest is a .... quarter   half   eighth   sixteenth   whole

15. 𝄢 This is a .... treble clef   bass clef   signature   rest   flat

16. ♪ This note is a .... half   whole   eighth   quarter   sixteenth

17. { This is a .... measure   brace   phrase   note   rest

18. 𝅗𝅥. This note is a .... dotted quarter   dotted whole   dotted half   dotted eighth

19. ‖ These two vertical lines are a .... measure   double bar   note   rest   clef

20. 𝄴 These numbers are called .... counting   time signature   rhythm   key signature

EL00245A